East and West

West

Home is the Best

An immigrant's Feelings and Views

A Poem

Muhammad Hanif

Dedication

*This work is dedicated to all those who leave their homelands **voluntarily**, to experience other cultures, societies, traditions in other countries, due to their desire to explore, or they do so in search of better opportunities, willingly and with the approval of the host country governments.*

Books by this Author

1. **Advice for Life**
2. **Clown and Frown**
3. **East and West – Home is the Best
    An Immigrant's Feelings and Views
    - A Poem**
4. **Everyday Poems**
5. **Living with a Stiff Spine – My Story
    of Coping with Ankylosing
    Spondylitis (AS)**
6. **Naughty Lioness**
7. **Short Stories Acrostic Way**
8. **Acrostic Stories Work Book
    Companion to Short Stories
    Acrostic Way**

Table of Contents

Introduction

Here is a story of an immigrant in the form of a poem.

The thoughts that are reflected here are a result of the experiences of the immigrant over the past several decades.

Enjoy the read.

Author

May 12, 2019

East and West

Home is the Best

An immigrant's Feelings and Views

I was born in 1942

In a land far away from Europe

During the World War II

Europe was being screwed

For the second time

By their own kind

That some called

"The Superior Kind"

In the first half of 20th century.

In case you do not know

"The Superior Kind;"

Germans were not the only one

"Who wanted a place in the Sun?"

They were simply left behind

By their neighbours

Who were neither friendly

Nor very kind; but

Were very selfish, and

Totally blind

Had no respect

For most of the mankind

In pursuit of their goals

For material kind; and

Who out smarted everyone

In atrocities

And despicable activities

Across the oceans.

English had great delusions too

About their superiority

And they still do

They were cold

And bold

And never hesitated

To express their views

Openly; and

Boldly

Either in speech

Or through their despicable deeds

Wherever they got a chance

Whether it was Lord Curzon

Or Churchill

They were from the same seeds

Screwing other nations

Was their mission

By their own admission.

But I was born

In an occupied land

Rich in cultures

Had plenty of Food and water

That attracted the vultures

From far off never heard lands

And from across the oceans.

My land was rich

In coal

And gold

To many it caused an itch

The European World schemed

Then set a goal

To get its hold

On our Gold

Body and soul.

I got carried away

And I digressed

I do not mean you any harm

My story has a great charm

So let me start again

That I was born

In an occupied land

Much bigger

Than the homeland

Of the Occupiers

Who occupied us

Just because

We were week

And meek

And many of us

Did not kill

Even animals

For meat

To meet

Our hunger needs.

We were humble

We had meagre needs

To live

And to please

Ourselves.

We had no greed

And no need

To bully anyone

Or everyone.

We were good people

Better than anyone

Or better still

Better than everyone.

We had plenty of food

In fact, plenty of every thing

We lived happily

There were some problems

But none were monumental

They were minor

As compared to the ones

Imposed on us

By the so called

Advanced people

The White people

Who were *advanced* indeed?

They were advanced;

In killing the innocent,

To meet their basic needs,

And their needs of greed.

It was difficult

To get rid of the aggressor

The occupier

But get rid of them

We did

At cost of life

And property.

We had a history

Full of mystery

When one occupier left

Then a new one came

For them it was a game

What a shame?

Then some of these

Mean men of greed

Whose ignorance

Was beyond belief

But had brains

Full of mischief

Fought

Amongst themselves

To decide

Who should leave; and

Who shall stay

To suck our blood

And quench their thirst

Till we were dead.

They sucked

Our blood

Our life

Our wealth; and

Destroyed

Our self esteem

Our ego

Our pride; and

Our values.

By the time they left

We were divided

Culturally;

Economically;

Mentally;

Philosophically;

Politically;

Physically;

Psychologically;

Religiously; and

Socially.

They sowed the seeds:

Of bribery;

Of corruption;

Of deception;

Of desperation;

Of dissention;

Of hate;

Of mistrust;

Of nepotism;

Of non-collaboration; and

Of separation.

They interfered

In our life styles; and

With our social customs.

They robbed us

Raped our civilization

And amazing it is

They still insist

To call themselves

Advanced

Civilized

Conquerors

Democratic

Helpful

Loving

Modern; and

Peaceful.

Whereas in reality

They were terrorists

Who were indeed:

Fear mongers

Greedy

Hateful

Jealous

Mean

Merciless

Ruthless

Scoundrels

Shameless

Terror generators

Vagabonds

Plain and simple.

Actually they were:

Super terrorists

Anarchists;

Arsonists;

Butchers;

Murderers;

Rapists;

Robbers;

Thieves; or

You may simply call them

Just plain sick bastards.

They thought

Everyone was an idiot

And forgot

To include themselves.

Finally,

Reluctantly,

They left in 1947

And left a mess behind

A chaos of a kind.

We managed;

To live;

Survive;

Progress; and

Pull ourselves together;

In all kinds of weather.

I went to school

Then to College

And University

Had great ambitions

Lots of energy; and

Enthusiasm

To work

And serve

My country

Full of diversity.

I found a job with a bank

And I am glad to tell you

That I enjoyed

Every moment

Working there.

I volunteered

When needed

To do social work

Provide free help

When and where needed.

I never felt the need

To go abroad

And seek

Anything indeed

And rated very poor on greed.

I had no desire

To go abroad

But I always met many people

Who were interested

In going to foreign lands.

Some were going to Middle East

To work for oil companies

Some were going to UK

Some others went to USA

To study

And then come back

Hoping

To get preferred for a job

With a better position; and

Higher pay.

Many were going to UK

Thinking that the old master

Will be delighted to see them

Will show some respect

They will have a better prospect.

Old master will reflect

Will be happy to select

For positions that need intellect.

They thought

They will be happy

To live and work there; and

To settle there.

I came across many of them

At my work in the bank

Where they came to get

A few Dollars; or

A few Pounds

Or some other

Foreign exchange

With weird names

Before they left.

Some wanted to chat

And to impress

Others wanted to rush

Got their job done

And left

And flew

Across the oceans

To lands of their dreams.

Few shared their fear

Of the unknown

Many were dreaming dreams

They were imagining things

They seemed to be hypnotized

Thinking of a fairy tale life.

They thought

Milk and honey was everywhere

In their desired destinations

Of foreign lands

And money grew on trees

And they were there

Just to pluck it

Or pick it up.

Many of them had an excuse

To leave their homeland.

Some did not like

The political system; although

They had no such ambition.

Many thought

They do not get the opportunities

That they deserved; although

Many people never honestly tried

Others were simply not qualified.

They all felt the strong need

To go to foreign lands

Where they want to be

And felt

That they should be there.

They were willing

To work hard

To work long hours; and

To do anything and everything

In those foreign lands.

They all thought

That they can live

Their full potential

In those foreign lands.

But Alas!

Little did they know?

Or pretended to ignore; that

There could be nothing

Farther than the truth

As the moment you land

In a foreign land

You become a foreigner;

A foreigner of the kind

That they do not want

To see going in front

Or walking behind.

They automatically think

That you are less than them

And doubt everything

About you.

They think:

Low of you

You cannot be trusted

Your educational credentials

Are false

Your skills

Are not good

Your character

Is questionable.

They think:

You will steal

You will lie

You will be dishonest

You will not be up to par

You cannot go far.

So they demean you

Hurt you

Insult you

Make fun of you

Mistreat you

Misguide you

Fool you.

Ever wondered

Why they think like that?

I think

It is because

They are reflecting

Their attributes on to you.

This is who they are:

Backstabbers;

Conniving;

Crooks;

Deceitful;

Liars;

Manipulative;

Mischievous;

Opportunist;

Scheming;

Unreliable; and

Untrustworthy.

They project all this

On to you.

They came for trade,

To buy; and

To sell,

In India.

They used crookery

Occupied the country.

Now when people come

From those once occupied lands

To their land

The land of the occupiers;

To visit;

To learn;

Or on immigration,

With their consent

And permission

They treat them

With contempt

No different

Than

When they occupied

Their homelands.

It is their mean deeds

They cannot become better

They will always be mean

Their morals were never high

And never will be.

It is in their make up

Some would call it genetic

Everything

Anything

They do

They think

Is better

Than you.

I decided one day

To find out

Why people like to go

To lands

Where people mistreat them.

Why some people praise

Some of the things about people

Who murdered our ancestors?

Why people talk about

Some Nations

In Europe

And in Americas

As advanced and interesting.

Although, I had a firm belief

That advanced Nations

Advance

Not by love

Or romance

Or by chance;

But by their ability

And skills

To kill

And instill

Tons of fear

Just like large animals do

To smaller ones.

Still being a man of science

I wanted to observe

Do my own research

Satisfy my own curiosity

So I applied for immigration.

I also found

Something

Interesting

Intriguing

Advanced countries needed

People with skills

In various fields

Like

Medicine; and

Computers

From countries

Known as backwards or

Developing; and

Countries

Generally disliked by the West

Except for tourism

And their fun and delight.

After a long process

I got processed

Got immigration papers

Left my homeland

Where I was comfortable

Very comfortable indeed

That I must repeat.

I expected

A smooth sailing

I thought

I will apply for a job

Prove my ability

My knowledge of skills

In the interview

Secure a position

Perform

Study the social

Cultural

Economic; and

Political environments

Draw some positive conclusions

And write about them.

But look

What I really found

I saw people

Running away from me

Trying to stay away from me.

No one wanted to talk

They just walked

Away from where I would be

No one would call

To socialize

Or for a job interview.

There were many jobs

Advertised in papers

But responses to them

Were never positive.

If someone ever called

For an interview

It was like an inquisition.

The interviewers were rude

Crude

Worst dudes.

It seemed

They wanted to torture

They were trying to find

Something

Where I would fail.

They were looking

For an excuse

To refuse.

But I also noticed

And was surprised

That if they were desperate

Then they would listen

Show interest

Smile

And hire.

Once hired

They were constantly nagging

To make sure

You are not at ease

And just do

What they please.

They will train

Their own kind

And polish their brain

But had no interest

For the excitement

In your veins.

It was clear, plain and simple

They had no interest

In your advancement.

They never hesitated

To fire you

Once their needs were filled;

But their own kind

Could stay

And get retrained.

I bought a house

Someone threw a mouse

I saw a shadow

I looked out of the window

I saw a woman in a red blouse

Whom, I thought

Had just lost her mouse

When I chased her

To give back her mouse

She was surprised

She could not believe

She rubbed her eyes

Twice

And said, "Why;"

"I could not understand,"

That she despised

My being on her street

She said that she does not like

Me, or my "Kind"

In her neighbourhood.

I read the local newspapers

They will have letters

Addressed to the Editor

Where people expressed

Hatred; and

Dislike

Of people like myself.

I wondered why

These bastards lie

They are the ones

Who kill and occupy

Lands of other people

And we came here in peace

But I realized

That they think

They have the might

And it is their right

To do as they please

Just like the jungle beast.

You pretend

To have human rights

That you violate

Left and right

With full force of your might

And take immense delight

Telling others

Not to be weaponised

While that is the only thing

You do day and night.

They pretend

To help

Collect funds

To send

To countries in ruins

Where they are the one

Causing the grief

And pain.

Let me tell you

A little bit about the women

Over there

There were many I met

Who did not have much;

Money in their purse

Or clothing on their body

The less they have

On their body

Happier they feel; and

Better it is for them

As it is fashion

Not any different than

Eve and Adam

Who did not have a Leaf

With a known Label

The less you can have

Greater will be your liking

You will have a bigger name

Followed by fame

There is no shame

That will be lame

It is a game

Staying ahead in nudity

Is the aim.

First there was progress

To clothe and shelter

Now the advancement

And the progress

Is in doing away with clothes

Have as few as possible

Flaunt your body

They have pride

In being naked

In being gay

Or lesbian

It boggles my mind

That you can be Gay

And still have kids

I think

These people are confused

With drugs and abuse

Their minds are clogged

That need to be flogged

Mentally;

Psychologically;

To clear the fog

That is logged

Deep inside their minds.

Most love dogs

Have laws

That protect dogs

More than the human beings

Now that is

Something I call

Flawed

But do not say anything

To dogs

Or you will be clawed

Or harassed.

They are also inefficient

And incompetent

Perhaps on a lesser scale

Than many other Nations.

I went to a Police Station

On a Friday

To request a service

That was requested

By some other agency

And for which there was a fee

As the service was not free

There were no people

At the station

Who needed any attention

The guy said,

"Come back on Tuesday"

"Or on Thursday"

We do not take such requests

On any other day.

To me it seemed

That if my car was stolen

He might say

Sorry

We cannot register

Any such complaints this day; as

We are doing

Only Roller Skates thefts today.

Doctors used to tell

The East Indian patients

In 1970s and 1980s

Sickness is caused

By your spices

And now they recommend

Use of every East Indian spice

For your better health and life

To everyone

Brown, Black, and Yellow

Or White.

Let me give you another story

About the stereotypes

Held by the ignorant Whites.

I bought a house

As wished by my spouse

We both went to see it

With the seller

For inspection

She looked at the kitchen

And asked

"What are those spots?"

On the ceiling;

The salesman smiled

And replied;

Madam, "Why do you pretend?"

"You know that!"

They are caused;

By your East Indian cooking.

The idiot soon realized

When my wife turned to him

Looked him in the eye

And said to him

That the house was brand new

And was never occupied

There was no stove

And no Frig in sight

But the stupid White

Never apologized.

I have never encountered

So much hatred and spite

Anywhere in my entire life

As demonstrated in a land

Which praises itself

Night and day long

How great it is

How safe it is

How compassionate it is.

May be all that is true

But not for everyone
Only for a chosen few.

People in power
Always advocate
That people should adapt
But I noticed
That seven million people
Whose ancestors
Were beaten in Europe
Were thrown out of India
Were punished in Indochina
And you should know
What happened to them
In North America
And now live in Canada
Have not adapted in 150 years
They have not learned
The language of the majority

They Cannot Decide

Whether to be independent

Or stay inside

Keeping the suspense

Staying on the fence

Gives them pleasure

Which is immense.

If it is a democracy indeed

Then they should do

What the majority does

Just shut up

And live like the rest

Without any fuss.

People talk about freedom

But they do not see

Freedom is never free.

You can vote

But that does not give you

The toast; or

The boat

In which you can float

And gloat.

You have to learn

To earn.

If you do not have money

You cannot buy honey

Or get Honey.

You need economic freedom

Which is a basic need

Only then and only then

You can have

Political ambition

Or enjoy

Political freedom.

The real question is

Why do in the West

The Governments

Allow people to come

In their countries

The people – the ones

Who are disliked

And despised.

You have people who think

That they can think!

Although, I have my doubts

As they have hate germs piled up

Like Brussel sprouts.

They call people names

Which will put decency to shame

They call them "Human Garbage"

Just because

Of the Colour of their skin

Or their religion

But they forget

That they have garbage

In plenty

But they cannot see

They are the garbage

Made of a strong base

From Western Europe

Then supplemented it

With imports

From Eastern Europe

Western Russia; and

Southern Europe

And wherever else

They could find it

And liked it

Preferred favourably

If it was white.

I think it is a plot

A game of good and bad Cop

West allows people to come

To their lands

To brag about

Their openness

Their hospitality

Giving a chance

To many of their people

To express their hostility

Keep their minds away

From political inefficiency; and

Incompetency.

They do it

To make their kind

Feel good

Keep busy

Confused; and

Fooled.

I now realized

Why people migrate.

People are influenced

By what they see

In the movies.

They see big houses

With cars

And beautiful women

Blondes

Tall

Thin and slim

With smiles

As long as a mile.

I saw good things

And bad things

In the new land

And I wanted to leave

But every time I tried

I found it hard

Because I was so tied

In routines of daily life.

Many convinced me to stay

And ride the tide.

Some people were nice

Not everyone was bad

Some looked glad

And were happy

Invited us to their yard

To share their lard.

I found it hard to leave

I felt that things might improve.

Home is where you are safe

And you feel at home

It can be anywhere

It does not have to be in Rome.

I finally left

And returned home

I was happy to be back

I was now happy

In my homeland

Things looked nice.

My perception was modified

Future looked shiny

Prospects seemed bright.

It was the start of a new life

I was now interested,

Motivated,

Enthusiastic; and

Eager,

To work harder to strive

And fight for my rights

I felt better than before

I had a greater focus

And direction

I was happy;

Joyful;

Pleased; and

Delighted.

Now that I am back here

Which is where I belong

As I was told that

Day and night long

By all those

In the foreign lands

I like to call them human beast

I must tell you

What I felt

But was afraid

To speak

In the land

That pretends

Freedom of speech

Which they exercise with pride

And is actually the freedom

To express "Hate"

But are quick to pound

On you for things they dislike

When you exercise

Your right

For freedom of speech.

I went to a job Councillor

A person who thinks

He or she knows

Better than you

What you can do

Who asked me a lot

About my background

And asked me

What I thought, I was best at.

She was not satisfied

With any thing

And everything I said

She had huge doubts

Perhaps that is the matter

She was made off.

I told her

I want to be a doctor

"Doctor – a medical doctor,"

She said

No! No! You cannot do that

You know nothing

About our culture

You are not a fit for that

But you can be a technician

Test urine, stools etc.

I said but I do not know

The culture of those things

As you told me

That I do not know

Much about culture

Culture is culture

Is not that true, I asked

You are a simple guy

She said

And you have a great body

You are tall and well built

You can work as a "Mover"

For a company that moves

Furniture and household goods

For people on the move.

I declined that

I said I like to join your army

And help you fight your enemies

She said that is not possible

You have to be a citizen

Come back when you are one.

I said, I want to be an air traffic
controller

She said that is a tough job

You have to score high on IQ

Aptitude test is tough too.

I said that I am well educated

I have advanced degrees

I am intelligent

I have ambition

I have good attitude

I have great aptitude

And I have lived

At great altitudes.

She smiled

She said that was what I think

It may be good

But it does not matter

What matters

Is what others think

And this other does not think

Well of you

You are different

Lot is needed to be done

Before you become the fit one.

She said good things

About the air traffic control.

She said that

I cannot be a doctor

Or an engineer

Or a professor

Or a lawyer

Unless I was educated here

And then I could be considered

To work in my field

My credentials may be great

But they were good only

For you to get here

There is not much else

We can do for you.

Take a job as a security guard

And consider yourself lucky.

I said that I will work in a bank

No, no such thing for you

Someone said sitting behind her

You guys do not speak

The way we do

I then got angry

Got up and left

And found a job in a bank

Where

There were too many people

Who thought

They spoke English

But I do not think

That they even knew

What they spoke

Was it Italian?

Or German!

I think it was Greek,

Even for the two Greeks,

Who always giggled,

On hearing others speak,

But these guys were White.

But the point is

You openly discriminate

On one ground or the other

You are not bold enough

Or strong enough

To tell and preach

What you really believe

But you are cold enough

To politely decline;

What may be?

Rightfully mine.

I think

You should be strong enough

To just stop people

Whom you do not like

To come to your country

It will be good for you

And for me and them too

You can keep your culture

And I do not have to study

Your culture from your waste.

I do not have to go

Out of the way

To prove

To be a fit

Among you; and

Your great collection

Of the misfits and unfits

And I do not have to worry

And you do not have to pretend

To fix and mend

The hate groups

That exist

Among you

Who try to harass people like me?

They flourish

And nourish

As they have the freedom

To destroy the freedom of others

Who may not have the freedom

To defend themselves

And if they tried

Then it will be considered

Unlawful

As taking the law

In your hands

And how can anyone like me

Know about them

As they all look alike

They are all White

Difficult to tell apart

Like grains of rice

Who just sit and lie.

They are a disgrace to the few

Who may be nice

And are in short supply.

Something should be done

To fix these mental warts

In your society

With pretend great hearts.

Now I know of many Doctors

From my country

Who would work as janitors

In your country

Hoping that this will improve

Their great credentials

That they already had

To study in your land

Study one more time

That they had studied before

So that they can earn a lot more

Than ever before.

But it is their choice

I find it disgusting

As you know that

No matter where you go

Two plus two is four

What I studied before

Was in no way inferior

As the books were similar

Most were written

By the so called

Western Experts.

I do not like

Your advice

I will not hide

But I will stay away from it

As far as I can

As I know, I can do better

On my own

Without your put downs.

I saw the process of elections

That you are so proud of

For Your Democracy

I did not find it any different

Then the one at home.

Politicians calling names

To their competition

One candidate insulted

His opponent

Focussed on the weaknesses

Never mentioned

His own strengths

And lost big time.

In another large democracy

One candidate insulted

Everyone

Men

Women

Colleagues

Neighbours

Friends

Foes

Other Nations

Religions

Particularly Muslim

Felt important

Felt that everyone loved him

Always insulted people

When in power

Did things

Whether they were needed

Or not.

I liked a lot of things

That I found in The West

They have a good outlook

You can call it structure

They are not anybody's friend

Although they do pretend

To lend

A hand to give

And the other one to grab.

Sometimes

They may give you cash

But then

They will come back

To you to trash.

They are wolves

In sheep's clothing.

They are always scheming

Have plenty of tools

And constantly building new ones

To control and fool

People everywhere

Except

Those in their gene pool.

People think good of them

Just because

They have a great outlook

They play sports

They made wars

Some with glory

Some with defeat

Massacred people like a beast

But many people still like them

Most even love them

They dress well; and

Look like model Nations

But are no models

Though they could be a model

They have good systems;

Like Education

Communications

Transportation

But they do not like people

People from many other Nations

But people like them

But when they approach them

Or they get to know them

They dislike them

Their manners are bad

It is indeed sad

But I am happy and glad

As I never liked them.

They are rude

Their manners are crude

They do smile

With a bitterness in their heart

They never went the extra mile

Except to kill and plunder

With great Thunder

Never did anything great

For people

Who were not their kind

Although sometimes

They smiled

But then captured

Indus and River Nile

They are the favourite

Of almost everybody

In Africa

In Asia

In China

In India

In Middle East

Where they have many priests

To spy and preach.

People loved their looks

The looks of their body

But they are not anyone's buddy

They dislike to be your buddy

They have a body

But they are no buddy.

Budding in that body

Were and still are buds

Buds of the bad kind

Of hatred that abounds

Of malice

That could fill many a challis.

There were buds found:

Of prejudice

Too intense to diminish

Of arrogance; and

Continued ignorance

Of false pride;

High on a horse ride

Of self-love

Of extreme narcissism

Mountains of indifference; and

Vocal criticism.

No body loved these buddies

From the heart

Who were no one's buddy

Who are no one's buddy

People always wondered

Why nobody likes these buddies

With a great body

These bodies did not learn

How to become a buddy

Because they have no sincerity

No interest in benefiting others

Except themselves.

You may be a lone country

Or a group of countries

You may be a small Nation

Or a large Nation

Be friendly

Be patient

Nothing lasts for ever

So enjoy and be happy

Help others, if you can

Else, just stay away

Out of the way

From the path of others.

Pursue your own happiness

Mind your own business

Let others do the same

In their own ways.

Many people I met

Some said

You speak good English

Some said

You are not like others

Some said

You are more liberal;

More liberal than others

Of your kind

Some said

You are lucky;

Lucky to be here

It is a great country

They said, "If I knew"

People sleep on the streets

In Bombay and Calcutta

Raped in Delhi

Washed by floods in Dhaka

Are robbed in Peshawar

Kidnapped in Kabul

Blown up in Baghdad

Killed in Quetta; and

Women cannot drive in Mecca.

People get beaten up; and

Go to jails

For religious beliefs

And class differences; but

Little did these idiots know?

That people in their own country

Are insulted

Humiliated

Dragged

From their seat on the plane

For which they have paid

Are refused a service

Are called names

Are beaten up

Murdered; and

Extremists of their own kind

Are provided protection

In the name of freedom

Or free speech

And good manners do not exist.

They can never comprehend

That we went to the best schools

With swimming pools

To cool

The teachers were no fools

Had plenty of teaching tools

Not only did we learn

Skills to earn

But learned proper language

Perhaps better than them

And many things about history

Physics and Chemistry

Business and Economics

And foreign policy

And other subjects

Many of these people

Did not know much

About their own land

And tried to be expert

On the lands of others

And affairs of other lands

They said the same things

To others like me

Whatever, they said to me.

They seemed to ignore

All those who beg

Sit on the side of the street

At entry or exits

Of bus and train stations.

Though I must admit

There numbers are few

But large numbers are found

At soup kitchens

And shelters.

The poverty in the West

Hides from the rest

Naked eye cannot see it

People like me are fooled by it

The poor guys live

Miserably just like anyone else;

Elsewhere on this planet.

I also found it amazing

Drug addicts abound

And get more attention

For their safety

And protection

Then many others

With noble intentions.

Interesting indeed

Are priorities

Of the governments

For the men on weed

Saving the overdosed addict

Is an act

Of great compassion indeed!

That it is only in the West

A two year old can shoot

His mother or his brother;

People can be dragged

From their seats on airplanes.

Some said

People in my country

Do not have as many cars

As they do in the West

They do not have much

Many do not have a Frig

Or a Stove

And other gadgets

That you consider

Necessities of West

That are luxuries in other lands

And many do not own homes

But they did not know

That most people

Do not have immense debts

Or owe money to banks

Or credit card companies

Most are debt free

And stress free.

They do not run

To see a psychologist

Or a therapist

When their cat dies

Or their dog does not bite

The neighbour they dislike.

They forget

That most people in the West

Have debts

Beyond belief

Bankruptcies are common

They live on credit cards

Many go bankrupt

Again and again; and

Live miserable lives.

Little do these ignorant know?

That everyone should know

People live differently

In different lands.

Women in the West

Have almost bare breasts

Naked legs

Seems like you cannot meet

Their clothing needs

But I know better than you

That people everywhere

Dress;

Meet; and

Greet

Differently.

They behave differently

They do

What they want

They are happy;

Happy with their differences

Generally they are nicer

Than people in advanced lands.

People like people

Some people dislike people

People are just people

People are honest

People are courageous

People are also dishonest

People are good in general

Some people are lazy

Some others are smart

Some are greedy

Some always just live

To eat

And fart

Some always play with darts

Some others are helpful

No two people are the same

Some have fame

And name

Some have shame

Some mind their own business

Many others intrude

In affairs of others; or

In whatever you do.

But somethings are universal

People here are more aloof

They are more self centered

Many are just hostile

Many are highly prejudiced.

When I was in my country

I could go

Wherever I wanted

Of course

There were pockets

Of crime here and there

Which I prudently avoided

But not a whole lot to fear

By just being there.

But my dear

The story is different here

There is fear every where

May be less here

And more there

One thing is very clear

That it is all fear

I called you dear

But believe me

You are no dear

Let me be very clear

From you, I too fear

I am more afraid

In your country

Then I was ever before

In my country

Which you cannot even pronounce

But when you hear the name

You just frown.

In your country

That you always call great

Several times a day

And tell several people

And tell me constantly

That I am lucky

To be here

In your country

Where I am full of fear

It seems to me

My every step is watched

My time everywhere is clocked

I feel

Everyone seems to dislike me

I see hate coming

Through their piercing eyes

It is difficult to walk

Even a hundred yards

Without being scared.

Some people shout obscenities

Some call names

From inside their cars

Some clowns

Just frown

When they pass by.

My boss

Who gave me a job

Asks me questions

On every action

As if I was a retard

Although to me

He looks like one.

He has a speech problem

Is lame in one leg

Which I thought

Was an injury from a war?

But he fell in a ditch

When he came drunk from a bar.

He is obese beyond belief

And I could see

Saliva coming from his mouth.

He is always drunk

In the afternoons

Smells awful after lunch

But I am sure

He feels great.

I did not say anything to him

He is the boss.

I think he was hired

Under the minority programme

Then he thinks that I am here

Because of my ethnicity

The real hire

Based on minority policy

Are people like him.

He is not a visible minority

But he is very visible otherwise

Because of many disabilities.

I have never seen

Much of any ability in him

Bur Eh! He is here

I cannot question

It is illegal.

Here is what I am going to do

I am going to tell you

As I see it

Because I feel

That someone

Must do

That has never been done

Before, by anyone

And what needs to be done

And done now.

Some people wondered

Why I do not eat lard

I tell them

I am afraid

That it will make me a retard

Just like my boss.

Listen, you all

And listen carefully

You are not great

Your country may be great

Although I doubt it

Because if you are not great

And many others

Who live here

And who are just like you

If they are not great

Then the collective

Cannot be great.

I hope you understand

The simple logic

Of what I just said

Most countries are great

In some way or the other

You are great in hate

You live in dreams

Your trousers are torn

At their seams

You have no knowledge

Of people and places

That you know names of

But nothing more

You have small minds

You have no knowledge

Of people of any kind

Although you claim

That you have good education.

You are lucky

That you have jobs

That you should not have

In the first place

You are rich

Rich in hate

Rich in prejudice

Rich in malice.

Your ancestors robbed

They raped

They destroyed

Countries in Africa

In Asia

In Americas

In the South

In the North

And in between

As if it was Halloween.

Now you pretend

To be the best human being

Humanist of all.

You terrorized the world

Now you say

The world does not behave

As it should

You talk about human values

Where were these values

Before now

You discovered them now

You became rich

At the cost of others.

You polluted the world

Now you talk about

Saving the environment.

I honestly believe; and

You have the proof

That you are the crooks

You are the vagabonds

You are the scoundrels

You are the mischief makers

You are the war mongers

You are the devils

You are the ones

That terrorize other Nations.

You talk about democracy

Where was it before

When you were plundering

When you colonised

Annihilated

Blasted

Enslaved

Evaporated

Mutilated

Terrorized

Vandalized

Humans and properties.

Now, some of you

Still do that

What they always did

Excuses have changed

You say you are afraid

Afraid of what?

I and many others

Find it hard to believe

That with a background of yours

You have any fear

Of anyone

Far or near

I think like many others do

You are paranoid

And are schizophrenic too.

You have nothing to fear

There is nothing real

You were afraid:

Of the communists;

Of the Chinese;

Of the Russians; and

Now you are afraid of Islam.

The rest of the world

Was afraid too

And is afraid even now

Of them and you.

But they did not resort to fight

But you did

Fight with all your hate

Fury and might

No one still knows

Who was wrong

And who was right.

You are always looking

To find excuses

To test and build

Your ability

To kill

And instill

Fear

And maintain your superiority

To destroy others.

Tell me the reasons

That led Alexander

To plunder

With great thunder

And go to India.

Why did they go there?

Dutch or Portuguese

Followed by the French

Who were then thrown

By the English; and

Why the English were there

To rob or teach democracy?

Or they were learning Hindi!

To help them expand their mind

Or they were doing charity work

For the humanity.

The English stayed there

They were there to rob

Kill

Loot

Massacre

Plunder

Rape

Subjugate; and

Feel good and great.

I wonder sometimes

In fact I firmly believe

That if there was no India

There would be no America

There would be no Great Britain

It is the Indian wealth and blood

That has kept the British alive

And helped them succeed

In Africa;

In Asia;

In Americas; and

Everywhere else.

People in general in the East

Love the West

And pretend to hate only

When the West bombs them

Then there is insecurity

West is selfish

Self centered

Hateful

Pretends to be loving

Merciful; and

Humanistic.

They bombed

Nation after Nation

In the Middle East

And then they say

They are afraid

And want peace.

You are selfish

You are mean

Beyond belief

You polluted

The atmosphere

You destroyed

The environment

Now you advocate

Global responsibility

For your acts of cruelty

And individuality

You want the world to cooperate

The same world

That you hate; and

You are willing to evaporate

With your nukes

If others ask you

To pay them their dues.

You cut your forests

In the name of progress

And development

Now you want others

To preserve

So as to help you.

You do not want

Other Nations to advance

Have a chance

To enhance

Their lives

That you regarded

And still do

As human garbage;

The "Garbage"

That helped you advance

That slaved for you

That suffered at your hands

That fed you

That bled for you

That begged you

To spare them

But you were drunk!

Very drunk indeed;

Also drunk with glory

And had a fogy mind

You were simply blind

And you have not changed

For better

You have new excuses

You propagate hate

Instill fear in others

And claim being afraid.

"Afraid of what," I say

The West bombed out Nations

Shame, Shame,

Unlucky are the Nations

In Middle East

Who bear the fury?

Fury of the Beast

And are called beast

By the beast

Who loves

Generating chaos

And mayhem

Shattering minds

Destroying places

Turning everything to pieces

Then tends to help;

Help restore peace.

Why the West

Cannot do their best

Simply leave the rest

To its rest

Rest in peace

And mind its own business

Simply stop shooting

Stop killing

Interfering

Stop propagating hate

Stop the people

Coming to the West

If it does not like them.

May be it is a genetic thing

It cannot help

It has to kill

Destroy others

This is the way

It is

It has been

And it will be

Come what may

It will not change

Change for better.

It is also genetic

For the guys in Middle East

To worship

And love the West.

They do not help their own

But go out of the way

To help the West

Be it an African

Or an Arab

Or a Chinese

Or an East Indian

Or a Middle Eastern

They just bite each other

But unite to help the White

And the West.

I went to Middle East

Saw some locals

Lick the White

Left and right

With delight

And always

Took their side

On matters wrong

And were never right

Hated their own kind

Who always supported

Their behind

Never told them

How much they appreciated

But always scolded them

For mistakes

They never made.

White was might

Even when they were wrong

Which was more often

Than

When they were right

Their behaviour was motivated

By the might

Of the White

By force; and

By being bully

To set things right.

The oilman did not pay

The Indian

The Pilipino

The Bangladeshi

The Pakistani

The Siri Lankan

But his coffers were wide open

For the bully White

Who was all phosphorus?

From West and North of Bosporus.

I painted a donkey white

And put it on an open site

In plain sight

By the road side

Next day there was a big crowd

And many were shouting loud

People were lined up in queues

The oilman wanted to lick it

The white wanted to save it

Take it

Protect it.

The White guys

In the oil lands of Middle East

Spent all day

Telling everyone

Except the locals

That the Oilman

Deserved to eat hay

Should not stay

And had no place

To live in the world of today.

The Oilman who was timid

And afraid of the White

Would gladly backbite

And told everyone

Except the White

That the White is just White

There is nothing inside

Give them some money

And you can get all the honey

They will sell you their mommy.

The Oilman said

They pay well to the White

Because it looks nice

To have them by their side.

You do not make them angry

Because they will eat you up

As if they could not find food

And were hungry

Then they can wage a war

From far

Funny they are

They send a plane to bomb

Then they send another one

To throw some food

And then again shoot

Killing is their game

Giving pain to others

Is their aim.

I saw a priest

At a book store

In the East

I asked him,

When is he going to Africa?

He was surprised

He said he never told me that

I said you are White

You must have committed

Some sins in the dark

And some in broad day light

And now you want forgiveness

What better way to find it

Other than by seeing the plight

And misery

Bestowed on the Black

By the White

And shed a tear or two

And have sex with a few

To leave behind some clue

For others

To view

That you were there

To view

The miserable many

Who do not have a Penny

And would love to work

As your Nanny.

In the West

The non-white gets treated

The worst

The White despises him

The fellow non-white

Treats him with contempt

That far exceeds

Contempt of the White.

The non-white gets beaten

In their homeland

By the Whites; and

In the West by the West

And also by his own kind

It boggles the mind

What is wrong?

With the non-white kind.

Here is my question to you

If you hate so much

Then why do you deal with people

You do not like

It seems that you cannot live

Without having people

That you can hate

Perhaps you feed on their plight

You do not have any might

You always do mean things

You always rush to kill them

You have

Weapons of mass destruction

You are not good in construction

That shows your judgement

And skills in love and protection

You cannot love human beings

Because

Then you will lose

Your ability to be bully.

Your soldiers go to war

They try to play smart

By playing games of war

In other people's yards

Destroy their homes

Kill their people

Claim PTSD

Why

No body tried

To find out the cause of PTSD

Perhaps they could not find

The donut

Or Shoverma; or the Kebob;

Of their favourite kind

Lost their mind

Or they stepped on their own mine

Which can kill them

Or made them blind

Or their wife or girl friend

Got pregnant, they left behind

By their friend

Or they committed a crime

That they cannot justify

In their mind.

After all I have said

I have sympathy for you

Because you are afraid

You are nervous

You fear

That you may lose

Your goose

Your moose

Your women

Who are mostly loose

Your ability to think

And to plunder

Due to abuse

Of drugs; or

Alcohol.

You banned cigarettes

And tobacco

But not alcohol

Now you want to decriminalize

Use of dangerous drugs

You are really psychotic people

Next will be to institutionalize

Rape

Murder

In your own land

Which now you practice

In other lands.

Some of you

In fact most of you

Talk about "Western Values"

But none of you

Have the ability to recognise

That your values were built

By the colonization of others

By the destruction of others

By robbing the others

And now

That times have changed

You cannot rob anymore

Although you try that still

But the rewards do not fill

Your till

They are a lot less

Then before

You cannot bask in the glory

Any more

As you did before

You feel awful

You talk about your virtues

Which are only virtual.

In the past

You openly robbed other nations

Now when you set up a factory

In one of those Nations

It is to give pennies in labour

And make huge profit margins

In your markets.

Some of you are now desperate

So they are selling

Citizenships of their country

What a clever gesture indeed!

It is a nice and polite way

To collect money and rob

People of their money

Then make them feel unwanted

And make their lives miserable

When they arrive.

Let me remind you; that

Betrayal;

Destruction;

Disrespect;

Hatred;

Hedonism

Hegemony;

Lies;

Racism; and

War;

Are the Western Values

Make no mistake about it

Admit it

Do something about it

Before you get consumed by it.

You talk about

Law and order

But you allow

Hate groups to flourish

In the name of free speech

You are mentally screwed.

A few years from now

You will be all drugged

You will be all gay

Or lesbians; and

Nude

You will be most advanced

To meet your needs

Just like Adam and Eve.

I think it is genetic

The West does not like

The Non-White

Who loves the White

And the West

I honestly believe is a parasite

That lives by taking the life

Of the girls and guys

In the East

Now tell me

Who is human? And Who is the beast?

Here is what I suggest

If you can digest.

>*Mend your ways*

>*Become human,*

>*Considerate; and*

>*Passionate.*

>*Love life*

>*Live; and*

>*Let others live.*

>*Live Peacefully*

>*Live without fear.*

>----- *The End* -----

Notes:

About the Author

Muhammad Hanif has various interests and he is passionate about writing. He also likes to travel. His educational background includes studies in science, psychology, computer science and business. He is working on several book writing projects which includes writing biography, self-help or advice, acrostic stories, some poetry and fiction.

Books by this Author

1. **Advice for Life**
2. **Clown and Frown**
3. **East and West – Home is the Best**
   An Immigrant's Feelings and Views
   - A Poem
4. **Everyday Poems**
5. **Living with a Stiff Spine – My Story**
   of Coping with Ankylosing
   Spondylitis (AS)
6. **Naughty Lioness**
7. **Short Stories Acrostic Way**
8. **Acrostic Stories Work Book**
   Companion to Short Stories
   Acrostic Way